Genre | Expository Text

Essential Question
How do we explain what happened in the past?

THE ANCESTRAL PUEBLOANS
BY KEN BENN

Introduction 2

Chapter 1
Who Were the Ancestral Puebloans?........... 4

Chapter 2
How Did They Live? 8

Chapter 3
Where Did the Ancestral Puebloans Go? 12

Conclusion................................ 16

Respond to Reading 18

PAIRED READ The Ancestral Puebloans Were Astronomers.................... 19

Glossary 22

Index 23

Focus on Social Studies 24

INTRODUCTION

The Ancestral Puebloans built cliff houses in Mesa Verde. The cliff houses are the **remnants**, or remains, of a Native American civilization. But in late 1290, the Ancestral Puebloans moved from the cliff houses.

The Ancestral Puebloans built these cliff houses in Mesa Verde. Today Mesa Verde is a national park in Colorado.

The Ancestral Puebloans had a rich **culture**. They were excellent engineers. They built tall buildings with hundreds of rooms. One *kiva*, or building, had a roof that weighed many tons.

The Ancestral Puebloans made designs on pottery and textiles. They also drew pictures on walls. The designs and pictures tell about their lives.

Archaeologists can learn a lot about Ancestral Puebloans by studying their houses. They also listen to the **oral histories** told by Ancestral Puebloan **descendants**, people who come from the same group of ancestors.

A long time ago, archaeologists started calling the Ancestral Puebloans the *Anasazi*. It is a Navajo word that can mean "the ancient ones" or "ancient enemies." But the Anasazi are the ancestors of modern Pueblo people. They call their ancestors *Ancestral Puebloans.* Today, some archaeologists use the name Ancestral Puebloans.

CHAPTER ONE
WHO WERE THE ANCESTRAL PUEBLOANS?

The Ancestral Puebloans built their homes in the American Southwest. But they were not the first Native Americans to live there.

Archaeologists and **historians** believe the first Native Americans were hunters and gatherers. They lived there between 13,000 B.C.E. and 6,000 B.C.E.

Early Native Americans started to farm between 6,000 B.C.E. and 500 B.C.E.

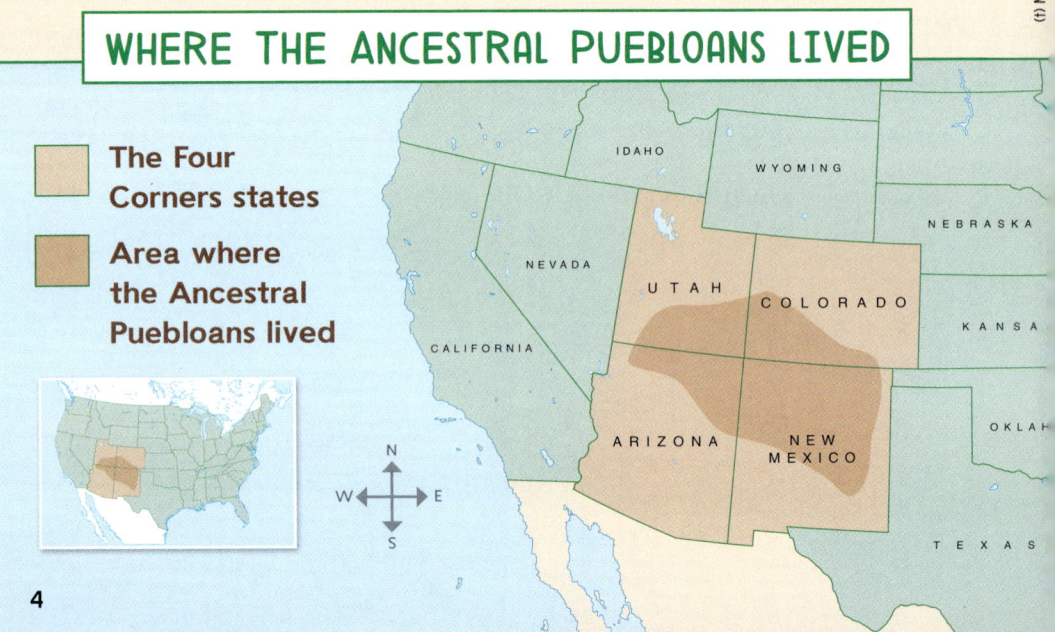

WHERE THE ANCESTRAL PUEBLOANS LIVED

- The Four Corners states
- Area where the Ancestral Puebloans lived

In the summer, the Ancestral Puebloans wore light clothing. In winter, they used cloaks and blankets.

Ancestral Puebloans were an **agricultural** people. They grew corn and other crops between 1,200 B.C.E. and 550 C.E.

METHODS THAT ARCHAEOLOGISTS USE

- Archaeologists dig ancient settlements to learn about ancient cultures. The most recent **artifacts** are found close to the top. The older artifacts are farther down.

- Archaeologists use radiocarbon dating to find the age of dead things. They measure how much carbon 14 remains in a dead thing to find its age.

- Archaeologists listen to oral histories. They are stories about the past that are told over many years.

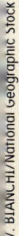

Archaeologists found many baskets in dry caves. The dry air in the caves helped to preserve the baskets. The baskets show the Ancestral Puebloans were very good artists and weavers. Archaeologists call this time the Basketmaker era.

Archaeologists believe the early Ancestral Puebloans built simple houses. The houses were round. They were built over holes in the ground.

From 500 C.E., the Ancestral Puebloans built houses that were larger. They lasted longer.

The early Ancestral Puebloans lived in simple, circle-shaped homes.

Around 750 C.E. to 900 C.E., the Ancestral Puebloans started to build with stone. Today, there are still stone buildings in Yellow Jacket, Colorado. Yellow Jacket was a large Ancestral Puebloan town. The town had more than 1,000 rooms. Many people lived in the town.

Water was important for farming. But the Ancestral Puebloans could not depend on rainfall. They needed to build their homes near water.

Later, the Ancestral Puebloans built larger cliff **dwellings**, or houses. The Cliff Palace in Mesa Verde is like apartment blocks. They were built into the sides of rock cliffs.

Many cliff dwellings can only be reached by ladders.

STOP AND CHECK

What are some Ancestral Puebloan things archaeologists have found?

CHAPTER TWO | HOW DID THEY LIVE?

Archaeologists study artifacts to learn about the people who made them. Many times, the artifacts are **fragments** of an object. But the pieces can give clues about how people lived.

The Ancestral Puebloans made different kinds of baskets. Many baskets were made to gather seeds, grains, and plants. Other baskets stored food. Some baskets were lined with a black substance called **pitch**. Pitch made the baskets waterproof. The baskets could hold water.

This basket was found in Mesa Verde National Park.

The Ancestral Puebloans started to make pottery around 600 C.E. Pottery was made in different places. For example, red pottery was made in southern Utah. The designs of the pottery help archaeologists date and identify, or to find out about, the pottery.

The Ancestral Puebloans designed pots with round bottoms. The pot could sit on three stones or in the sand.

MUG HOUSE

Mug House was built under a huge rock in Mesa Verde. It is called Mug House because many whole and intact pottery mugs were found there.

The Ancestral Puebloans built a large reservoir below Mug House. The reservoir collected the water that ran off the rocks on top.

The cliff dwellings at Mesa Verde are some of the best preserved cliff dwellings in North America.

9

Archaeologists have studied large pueblos, or towns, and cliff dwellings. They believe the Ancestral Puebloans worked and **socialized**, or met friends and family, in large yards outside. Piles of old corncobs were found in some houses. This shows that agriculture was important to the Ancestral Puebloans.

Sometimes, there was a lot of rain for farming. But some years there was no rain. So the Ancestral Puebloans built dams and reservoirs to control the water they needed.

This photograph shows an aerial view of what the ancient Chaco Canyon settlement looks like today.

Chaco Canyon in New Mexico was another Ancestral Puebloan center. The Ancestral Puebloans used huge logs to support the roof of a large kiva. But there were no trees near Chaco Canyon. Where did the logs come from?

Scientists studied a chemical **element** in the old logs. They discovered that the trees came from more than 50 miles away.

The logs were long and heavy. Thousands of logs were brought to Chaco Canyon. Archaeologists know the Ancestral Puebloans did not have oxen or donkeys. People moved the logs. This shows the Ancestral Puebloans worked well together.

> **STOP AND CHECK**
>
> How do archaeologists figure out how the Ancestral Puebloans lived?

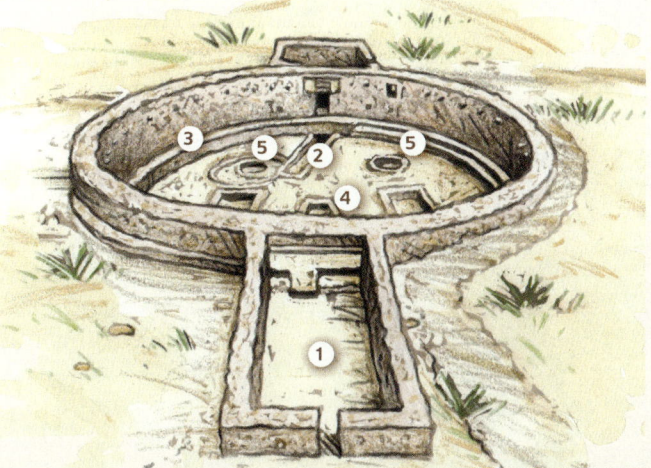

CASA RINCONADA KIVA, CHACO CANYON

1) Entrance
2) Under-floor passage
3) Bench
4) Firepit
5) Pits for roof supports

11

CHAPTER THREE
WHERE DID THE ANCESTRAL PUEBLOANS GO?

Archaeologists have wondered why the Ancestral Puebloans moved from their communities and went to other places.

Native American oral histories tell about droughts in the 1100s and 1200s. Scientists have also studied tree rings. The studies show there were droughts at that time. So the Ancestral Puebloans moved to places with water.

Today you can take a tour at Chaco Canyon. A guide tells about the amazing Ancestral Puebloan culture. The guide gives information from Native American oral histories and studies by archaeologists.

Native American oral histories also tell about violence in some communities. Archaeologists have also found bodies that were not buried in the **traditional**, or usual, way.

CLUES FROM THE RINGS OF TREES

Every year a tree makes a ring of new growth between the old wood and the bark.

Changes in temperature and rainfall affect how fast a tree grows. As a result, the size of the tree rings changes.

Scientists study tree rings to learn about the climate in the past. They can identify warm, cold, or wet years.

Narrow tree rings show that the climate may have been colder in the past.

Where did the Ancestral Puebloans go when they left their homes? Most modern Pueblo people living in New Mexico and Arizona are descendants of the Ancestral Puebloans.

Native American oral histories tell about how the Ancestral Puebloans moved to other areas. They may have also **merged**, or joined, with other Native American groups.

Some archaeologists believe the Ancestral Puebloans of Chaco Canyon moved more than 380 miles south. Today, this area is in Mexico.

Pueblo descendants of the Ancestral Puebloans still live in the American Southwest. Some still live in their native pueblos. Others live in nearby towns and cities. Some live in other states and countries. No matter where the people live, they are always welcome home to their communities.

STOP AND CHECK

What made the Ancestral Puebloans leave their homes?

The Taos Pueblo in New Mexico is a National Historic Landmark.

CONCLUSION

Archaeologists gather artifacts and use scientific methods to **reconstruct** the history of the Ancestral Puebloans. They also listen to modern Pueblo people's oral histories, traditions, and values to better understand the Ancestral Puebloans.

Native Americans have a strong connection to their lands. Most archaeologists believe that by 500 C.E., the Ancestral Puebloans settled across the Southwest. They built simple houses and farmed.

Over the next 250 years, Ancestral Puebloans built large stone buildings. They designed baskets and pottery.

During the late 1200s, droughts and possible violence made the Ancestral Puebloans leave their communities. They moved to different areas. Ancestral Puebloan descendants today are members of about two dozen different Native American pueblos and tribes.

Today, Native Americans continue their ancestors' traditions and ceremonies while also looking forward to change.

Respond to Reading

Summarize

Use important details from *The Ancestral Puebloans* to summarize the text. Information from your graphic organizer may help you.

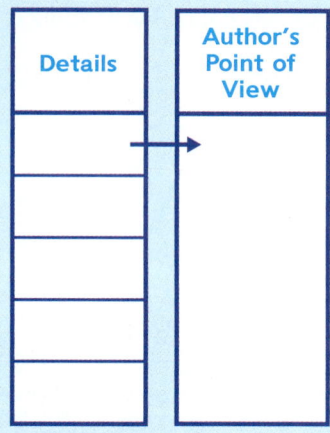

Text Evidence

1. What is the author's point of view about the Ancestral Puebloans? Give examples of words and descriptions the author uses that show his point of view. **AUTHOR'S POINT OF VIEW**

2. Reread page 8. What does the word *substance* mean? What clues help you figure it out? **VOCABULARY**

3. Write about the author's opinion of the skills of the Ancestral Puebloans and their descendants on pages 8 and 9. Include facts that show the author's point of view. **WRITE ABOUT READING**

Genre | Persuasive Article

Compare Texts

Read about the theory that the Ancestral Puebloans were astronomers.

THE ANCESTRAL PUEBLOANS WERE ASTRONOMERS

We know that the Ancestral Puebloans were farmers. Were they also **astronomers**?

Many ancient people studied the sky. They looked at the position of the sun to help them plant crops. The Ancestral Puebloans may have used astronomy to farm, too.

In 1977, an artist was studying rock art at Chaco Canyon, New Mexico. She saw something interesting. A beam of sunlight shined on spiral symbols on the rocks. She decided to study the rocks in different seasons.

The beam of light is called the "Sun Dagger." It cuts the spiral in half.

At summer **solstice**, she saw a beam of sunlight divide in half a spiral symbol on a rock.

At the spring and fall **equinoxes**, the artist saw a beam of sunlight divide a smaller spiral nearby. And on the winter solstice, two sunlight beams lined up on the edges of the large spiral.

But some archaeologists did not believe that these were Ancestral Puebloan tools to study the sky.

However, there are other Ancestral Puebloan structures that seem to measure the time of the year. At Casa Rinconada, in Chaco Canyon, the sun will shine on certain windows at different times of the year.

There is a rock painting in Chaco Canyon with three symbols: a star, a moon, and a handprint. The positions of the symbols suggest the Ancestral Puebloans were recording the Crab Nebula. The Crab Nebula first appeared around 1054 C.E.

Many people believe these Ancestral Puebloan rock paintings show the first appearance of the Crab Nebula.

Ancestral Puebloan sites and the oral histories of modern Pueblo people tell how the Ancestral Puebloans studied the movements of the sun, stars, and planets. The evidence shows the Ancestral Puebloans were astronomers.

Make Connections

How does the author explain what the artist saw at Chaco Canyon? ESSENTIAL QUESTION

After reading *The Ancestral Puebloans* and *The Ancestral Puebloans Were Astronomers,* what can you conclude about these ancient people? TEXT TO TEXT

Glossary

agricultural *(a-gri-KUHL-chuhr-uhl)* to do with farming *(page 5)*

artifacts *(AHR-ti-fakts)* any objects made by humans; for example, tools, pottery, or jewelry *(page 5)*

astronomers *(uh-STRAH-nuh-muhrz)* people who study the night sky *(page 19)*

culture *(KUHL-chuhr)* the lifestyle, practices, and beliefs shared by people who live in the same place or time *(page 3)*

element *(E-luh-muhnt)* a simple chemical substance, such as oxygen *(page 11)*

equinoxes *(EE-kwuh-nahks-iz)* the two times each year (about March 21 and September 21) when day and night are of equal length *(page 20)*

oral histories *(OR-uhl HIS-to-reez)* stories told about the past that are passed along for many years *(page 3)*

pitch *(pich)* a black, sticky substance that is waterproof *(page 8)*

solstice *(SOHL-stuhs)* the time halfway between the spring and fall equinoxes (about June 21 and December 21 each year) *(page 20)*

Index

agricultural culture, *4, 5, 7, 8, 10, 16, 19*
astronomy, *19–21*
baskets, *6, 8, 15, 16*
Chaco Canyon, *10, 11, 12, 14, 20, 21*
  – Casa Rinconada, *11, 20*
  – rock painting of the Crab Nebula, *21*
housing
  – buildings, *3, 6, 7, 16*
  – cliff dwellings, *2, 7, 9, 10*
  – pueblos, *10, 15*
kiva, *3, 11*
Mesa Verde
  – cliff dwellings, *2, 7, 9*
  – Cliff Palace, *7*
  – Mug House, *9*
modern Pueblo people, *3, 14, 15, 16, 17*
moving from the communities
  – reasons why, *12, 13*
  – where they went, *14*
pottery, *3, 9, 16*
Taos Pueblo, *14, 15*
tree rings, *13*
Yellow Jacket, *7*

Focus on Social Studies

Purpose To explore Ancestral Puebloan culture

What to Do

Step 1 Work as a group. Decide if you want to make a model of an Ancestral Puebloan building, basket, or pot. Then research your subject.

Step 2 Make careful drawings and measurements of your object. Write a list of materials you will need to make the model.

Step 3 Gather your materials. Use your drawings, and photographs from *The Ancestral Puebloans*, to make and decorate your model. Make the model as accurate as possible.

Step 4 Present your model to the class. Explain what you made and why you chose it. What did you learn? How did making your model make you feel connected to the Ancestral Puebloans? Now display your model in your classroom.